P9-CMQ-393

Presented to

Tammy C. Pitcher

from

Donna L. Pitcher

2010

A Christmas
greeting
from the
heart.

Joy Notes at Christmas

Just for You, Daughter

Illustrated by Beth Yarbrough

COUNTRYMAN

Project Editor—Terri Gibbs

Designed by Left Coast Design, Portland, Oregon

ISBN: 0-8499-9538-8

www.jcountryman.com

Printed in China

A message of
good cheer at
this happy time
of year.

The hope of Christmas fills the air...

while joy is scattered everywhere!

Christmas cookies,
of ginger
and spice,
baked with care
for someone
so nice!

Trees in colored
candy lights,
Wreaths with small
red bows,
A daughter who's
a great delight...
no wonder my joy
overflows!

Here are some
of the things that
make you special:

You Are A Child
of God

You Were born to
Glenn and Donna Pitcher

You Are Kind, generous,
and thoughtful

Hearts
go home at
Christmas,

home
to those
we love.

You are
God's gift
to me!

I can't
give you
my love
in a box
tied up
with
a bow...

but it's here
in my heart
every day
of the year.
I wanted
you to know.

A gift can be large,
A gift can be small,
but a gift
wrapped in love
is the best
gift of all.

All the
bells of
heaven
chime...

bringing joy
at Christmastime.

If I could give you
any gift in the world,
I'd give you the gift of:

Your father to be there for Christmas and every day

The
Christmas
star
spreads
love near
and far.

A Christmas prayer for you:

I Pray that You Believe in Jesus Christ And that you hold Him Close in Your heart. Place God first in Your life always. I thank God that You loved Your father And You Keep his memory near. I Thank God for You – Tamara C. Pitcher

In Jesus Name, Amen

May the wonder
of Christmas
bring joy
to your heart...

as you

bring joy

to mine!

With much
love

Mom

Forever

12/25/2010